Author: Jasper Montgomery

ISBN HARDBACK: 978-9916-90-830-3

ISBN PAPERBACK: 978-9916-90-831-0

Incantations at Sea

Whispers dance upon the tide,
Mysteries in waves abide.
Salted air and twilight's grace,
Enchantments form in ocean's space.

Stars reflect in waters deep,
Siren's songs, a spell to keep.
Moonlit paths where shadows weave,
Heartfelt truths that never leave.

Currents twist and spirits soar,
Echoes call from distant shore.
Voices lost in foamy sighs,
Guiding hearts with ancient ties.

Teardrops of the Moon

Silver beams through velvet skies,
Whisper softly, daylight dies.
In the night, a sorrowed glow,
Tales of love the shadows know.

Each teardrop holds a secret bright,
Reflections of the quiet night.
Lovers' dreams in silver light,
Fading fast with morning's flight.

Hope and longing, intertwined,
In the dark, both heart and mind.
Softly weep, oh moonlit sphere,
For every ghost that lingers near.

Veiled Horizons

Misty shrouds conceal the dawn,
Whispers of the night drawn long.
Hearts alight with dreams untold,
In the haze, the world unfolds.

Colors blend in twilight's art,
Secrets held within the heart.
Veiled horizons beckon near,
Promises of what we hold dear.

Glimmers of a brighter fate,
In the silence, we await.
Adventure calls beyond the mist,
Life's embrace, a gentle tryst.

Midnight Currents

In the deep, where shadows play,
Time is lost, and dreams drift away.
Midnight currents pull me close,
In their depths, I find my most.

Stars above like lanterns gleam,
Guiding souls through every dream.
A dance of waves, a siren's call,
Echoes linger, softly fall.

Whispers float on midnight air,
Secrets shared, without a care.
In this realm, both wild and free,
I surrender, lost at sea.

Beneath the Shimmering Veil

In twilight's glow, the whispers call,
Beneath the veil where shadows fall.
The stars align in gentle grace,
A canvas painted, time and space.

Through silver mist, the secrets weave,
A tapestry for hearts to leave.
In silken threads, our dreams ignite,
Beneath the shimmer, pure delight.

The Dark Dance of Water's Edge

Where water meets the night's embrace,
The dark reveals its hidden face.
A dance of shadows, cool and deep,
The secrets that the currents keep.

Rippling dreams in moonlit flow,
The ebbing tide begins to show.
With every wave, a ghostly twirl,
The dark dance spins, our thoughts unfurl.

Tempest of Dreams Unfurled

In stormy skies, the visions rise,
A tempest fierce, with burning eyes.
We chase the wind, our spirits soar,
In swirling chaos, we explore.

The heartbeats clash, a thunder's roar,
While hopes and fears collide once more.
In shattered dreams, we find our way,
Through tempest's grip, we greet the day.

Starry Veils of the Abyss

In endless night, the stars are spun,
A tapestry where dreams begun.
Veiled in whispers, shadows play,
In the abyss, we drift away.

With every twinkle, secrets gleam,
A universe that dares to dream.
Through cosmic paths, our hearts take flight,
In starry veils, we chase the light.

Twilight's Glistening Threads

In hues of gold, the daylight fades,
Whispers of dusk, in silence wades.
A canvas brushed with softest light,
The stars awake, to greet the night.

In shadows cast, the dreams unite,
Each fleeting hope, a spark of bright.
The moon, a guardian in the dark,
Guides wandering souls with gentle spark.

Silken threads of twilight weave,
Nature sighs, as hearts believe.
With every breath, a tale unfolds,
In twilight's arms, the world enfolds.

So let us dance on twilight's stage,
Where light and dark blend, age to age.
In this embrace, we find our place,
In glistening threads, we find our grace.

Tides of Reflection and Reverie

At dusk, the waters softly sway,
Whispers of dreams, they drift away.
Reflecting visions, lost and found,
In silken ripples, thoughts abound.

The moonlight kisses the endless sea,
A dance of shadows, wild and free.
Each wave a story, deep and grand,
In luminous glow, we understand.

Thoughts alight on gentle tides,
With every swell, a heart abides.
In silent moments, we can see,
The tides of reflection, setting free.

Let waves carry us to the shore,
In reverie, we seek for more.
A timeless journey, hand in hand,
Through tides of dreams, we glimpse the land.

Ebbing Secrets

Beneath the surface, darkness plays,
In hidden depths, the shadow stays.
Whispers of time, they softly flow,
Ebbing secrets, true and low.

The moonlit waves, a shrouded veil,
Each crest and trough, a ghostly tale.
With every rise, the past returns,
Ebbing secrets, the heart still yearns.

In salty air, the echoes breathe,
The ocean's heart, the soul's reprieve.
Nature holds what we can't speak,
Ebbing secrets, both strong and weak.

So let the tide reveal its lore,
In silent whispers, evermore.
For in the depths, we find what's real,
Ebbing secrets, the soul can heal.

Nocturnal Tides

The night descends, a velvet shroud,
In shadows deep, the stars grow loud.
A symphony of twinkling lights,
Bringing warmth to the coldest nights.

The ocean sings with lullaby,
As moonlit waves cradle the sky.
In this embrace, the world unwinds,
Nocturnal tides, where peace unwinds.

Each wave a pulse of ancient lore,
Whispers of dreams along the shore.
With every tide, the stories flow,
In nocturnal depths, our spirits glow.

Let's lose ourselves in twilight's grace,
In nocturnal tides, we find our place.
A dance of shadows, strong and free,
In night's embrace, just you and me.

Quietude in the Moon's Laughter

In stillness, shadows play,
A silver glow leads the way.
Crickets sing in gentle sway,
Night unfolds in soft array.

Stars glisten like distant dreams,
Whispers float on timid beams.
The world stirs in silent seams,
While peace reigns, or so it seems.

Every breath a secret sigh,
Beneath the vast, unchanging sky.
In the moon's soft lullaby,
Time drifts softly, passing by.

In this moment, hearts renew,
Wrapped in night's tender hue.
Here, joy bloomed from starlit dew,
Quietude in the moon's view.

The Drift of Night's Solitude

The night drifts slowly, pale and wide,
A canvas stretched, where dreams abide.
Stars twinkle like whispers, side by side,
In solitude, where secrets hide.

The wind carries a lover's tune,
Underneath a watchful moon.
In shadows deep, hearts commune,
Dancing softly, like a swoon.

Ghostly echoes of days gone past,
Frame the stillness, shadows cast.
Every heartbeat, a fleeting gasp,
In this night, where moments clasp.

Solitude wraps like a cloak,
With every sigh, a new word spoke.
In the stillness, dreams evoke,
The drift of night, softly bespoke.

Currents of Forgotten Whispers

Beneath the waves, secrets flow,
Currents dance, soft and low.
Words once lost begin to glow,
In the depths, echoes grow.

Fragments of stories intertwined,
Voices in the silence aligned.
In the dark, the past redefined,
As memories, blurring, unconfined.

Through the tide, whispers weave,
Tales of sorrow, tales that grieve.
Yet hope emerges, none believe,
Currents hold what hearts perceive.

Time, a river that shall not cease,
Carrying dreams toward peace.
In forgotten whispers, release,
Currents of silence find their lease.

Potion of Dusk and Deep

As the sun dips below the crest,
Colors blend, evening's guest.
Whispers of twilight softly rest,
In the potion of dusk, we're blessed.

Deepening shades of ruby and gold,
Stories of night, yet untold.
Beneath the stars, our hands hold,
Magic alive, dreams unfold.

The air hums with a vibrant tune,
As the moon rises bright, a boon.
In this soft embrace, hearts swoon,
Potion of dusk, sweetly strewn.

In the quiet, the night draws near,
An alchemy only few can hear.
In stillness, we shed our fear,
Dusk, deep magic, ever clear.

Lost in the Ink

Words spill like secrets, a silent scream,
Pages whisper softly, weaving a dream.
Inkblots of worry, shadows of fear,
In this quiet chaos, the heart draws near.

Pen dances wildly, tracing the night,
Thoughts fray and twist, caught in their flight.
Stories awaken, rich and profound,
In the lost in the ink, freedom is found.

Shadows Beneath the Tide

Whispers of water, a lullaby sweet,
Moonlight entangles, where darkness will meet.
Beneath the surface, secrets reside,
Shadows are dancing, in ripple and glide.

Currents are weaving, tales of the deep,
Mysteries linger, the ocean will keep.
Bubbles of laughter and sighs lost to time,
In shadows below, the depths quietly rhyme.

The Calm Before Dusk

Golden rays linger, a soft, tender light,
Birds sing their last song, preparing for night.
The world holds its breath, in tranquil embrace,
As day slips away, leaving only a trace.

Trees whisper secrets, in the hush of the hour,
The sky painted soft, a delicate flower.
Moments hang still, like a pause in a prayer,
In the calm before dusk, magic fills the air.

Dreaming in Blue

In a world painted azure, dreams take their flight,
Waves of imagination, dancing in light.
Clouds drift like dreams, soft and surreal,
Whispers of blue skies, eternally real.

A calm ocean's depth, where wonders unfold,
Stories of sky, in hues rich and bold.
Each heartbeat a wave, in rhythm so true,
In the gentle embrace, we're dreaming in blue.

The Abyssal Call

In depths where silence reigns, a voice does rise,
An echo lost in time beneath the skies.
A call that beckons with a chilling tune,
A whisper of the deep, a haunting croon.

The waters shudder, dark and wide,
With secrets held, where shadows hide.
The siren's song pulls hearts to roam,
To seek the place that's far from home.

Beneath the waves where dreams may dwell,
Lies an enchantment, a mystic spell.
To answer may mean to drift away,
To lose the light, to greet the gray.

Yet I am drawn, can't help but fall,
Into the void, the abyssal call.
A parting glance at the world above,
Then sinking down, into the deep I love.

Lament of the Dusk

As day concedes to evening's sigh,
The colors bleed against the sky.
A wistful breeze whispers true,
A soft lament for the fading hue.

The sun dips low, a golden ball,
Casting shadows long, a gentle thrall.
Each moment shared is one to hold,
Yet twilight speaks of stories old.

In every dusk, a promise lost,
Of dreams that come at a deep cost.
The stars awake in mournful grace,
They twinkle tender in their place.

Yet here I stand, my heart in tow,
As night descends, and feelings grow.
For mourning light means hope to find,
In every dusk, a love entwined.

Shadows on the Tide

The tides retreat, a dance of fate,
Leaving whispers of ghosts that wait.
In moonlit pools, reflections gleam,
Where shadows linger, lost in dream.

Waves reach out with gentle hands,
Caressing shores of forgotten lands.
The night unfolds its cloak so wide,
As darkness yawns, and fears abide.

Footprints traced in silver sand,
Stories woven, hand in hand.
Each shadow speaks in soft, low tone,
Of wanderers lost, forever alone.

Yet the tide returns with a knowing grace,
To wash away each trace, each face.
And still they dance in twilight's glow,
Those shadows call, a sweet hello.

Stillness in the Deep

In stillness deep, the ocean breathes,
A world concealed, where time weaves.
A tranquil place, where sorrows cease,
And in the void, I find my peace.

The surface calm, a mirror clear,
Reflects the stories I hold dear.
Below the waves, a secret keeps,
In silence vast, my spirit leaps.

Embraced by depths, I drift and sway,
Where currents cradle, fears decay.
In whispers soft, the water sings,
A lullaby of ancient things.

I lose myself in twilight's gleam,
Embraced by shadows, caught in dream.
Stillness reigns, my heart, it sleeps,
In tranquil depths, where magic seeps.

Silent Surge

Beneath the waves, the whispers sigh,
A hidden current, soft and shy.
The moon hangs low, a silver grin,
Embracing depths where dreams begin.

Each crest and trough tells tales untold,
Of kingdoms lost and treasures bold.
With every pulse, the ocean breathes,
In silent strength, its secrets weave.

The shadows dance in twilight's glow,
As gentle tides begin to flow.
Within the depths, the silence reigns,
A soothing balm for weary brains.

In stillness found, the heart can soar,
Through silent surges, evermore.

Luminescent Depths

In glowing hues, the ocean glints,
Where creatures glide and time hints.
A world of wonders, deep and wide,
In luminescent depths, they glide.

Bioluminescence paints the night,
With every pulse, they share their light.
Below the surface, life ignites,
A dance of colors, pure delights.

Starry skies meet ocean's floor,
In hidden realms, there is much more.
A journey into the shining blue,
Revealing secrets, old and new.

As waves embrace the darkened shore,
The depths invite, forevermore.

Ocean's Lullaby

The gentle waves hum soft and low,
A lullaby from far below.
Caressing shores with tender grace,
In ocean's arms, we find our place.

The azure depths cradle our dreams,
As moonlit paths weave silver streams.
With whispered tones, the sea confides,
As time dissolves in flowing tides.

Echoes of love and loss in air,
In every swell and undertow, we share.
The lullaby drifts into night,
A soothing balm, so warm, so right.

Rest easy now, let worries fade,
In ocean's heart, be unafraid.

Shimmering Dusk

As daylight wanes, the world aglow,
In shimmering dusk, soft colors flow.
The horizon blurs, where oceans meet,
A tranquil canvas, pure and sweet.

Golden hues blend with shades of blue,
A fleeting moment, ever true.
Whispers of night begin to stir,
As stars awaken, bright confer.

The tide retreats, a graceful sway,
In dusk's embrace, the world will play.
With every breath, the beauty stands,
A treasure found in fleeting sands.

So linger here, let worries part,
In shimmering dusk, unite the heart.

Tides of Moonlit Secrets

Under the silver glow so bright,
Whispers dance on waves at night.
Secrets carried on the breeze,
Lost in soft and swaying trees.

Footprints fade upon the shore,
Unraveled tales of those before.
The moonlight bathes the world in dreams,
Where nothing is as it seems.

A gentle tide that ebbs and flows,
Revealing what the darkness knows.
In shadows deep, the visions play,
As night meets dawn, a brand new day.

In every rise and every fall,
The ocean speaks, a timeless call.
Of journeys vast and love once lost,
The tides of secrets bear their cost.

Echoes Beneath the Stars

Beneath the cosmos, vast and wide,
Soft echoes of the night reside.
Songs of old, in silence weave,
Tales of wonder, if you believe.

The stars, they spark in rhythmic dance,
Inviting whispers, a fleeting chance.
Each twinkle tells a story grand,
Of love, of loss, of time's own hand.

In stillness, hearts hear distant calls,
A harmony that gently falls.
With every sigh, the night will share,
The echoes drifting through the air.

Hold tightly to the dreams you seek,
In starlit realms where spirits speak.
For in the dark, hope finds its way,
Guiding hearts till break of day.

Whispered Currents in the Night

Beneath the cloak of twilight's hue,
Currents whisper secrets true.
In murmur soft, they call your name,
Each ripple carries hints of flame.

Stars above in silence blink,
Watching as the shadows sink.
With every tide, the stories blend,
Embracing night as faithful friend.

The water flows, a timeless sigh,
While dreams take wing, prepared to fly.
In whispered tones, the night avows,
A canvas drawn beneath the boughs.

Spaces filled with magic's grace,
In every ripple, there's a trace.
Of love and sorrow intertwined,
In whispered currents, hearts aligned.

Lullabies from the Deep

From ocean's heart, a song will rise,
Lullabies beneath the skies.
Softly sung by waves that sway,
Embracing dreams till break of day.

In depths where silence holds the sway,
Gentle whispers guide the way.
Each note a touch, a tender care,
In watery realms, free from despair.

The melody of night takes flight,
Cradled in the arms of night.
With every wave, the stories blend,
A nurturing bond, a mystic friend.

So close your eyes and drift away,
To lullabies the sea will play.
In dreams, the deep will softly keep,
The secrets held, in peace, you'll sleep.

Rhythm of the Deep

In shadows where the currents flow,
The secrets of the deep they know.
A dance of bubbles, soft and light,
In twilight's grip, they weave the night.

Echoes of dreams beneath the waves,
Whispers of past, the ocean saves.
Mysteries rise with every tide,
As stars above in silence bide.

A pulse of life in deep blue sea,
The rhythm calls, it calls to me.
With every swell and every crest,
The heart of ocean finds its rest.

Together, where the wild things dwell,
In waters deep, there lies a spell.
For in the depths, life sings a song,
A melody where we belong.

Midnight's Serenade

The moonlight pours like silver streams,
A calming quilt beneath our dreams.
In velvet night, the world awakes,
With whispered tunes that twilight makes.

Soft shadows dance on silent streets,
While time, it slows with gentle beats.
Each star adorned, a fleeting spark,
As lovers meet within the dark.

The air is thick with sweet perfume,
Beneath the trees, in nature's womb.
A serenade, so pure and clear,
Invokes the heart to draw you near.

In midnight's grasp, we find our place,
A timeless bond, a soft embrace.
When dreams entwine, the night extends,
In lullabies, we find our friends.

Enigmatic Tides

The ocean holds a mystic spell,
In whispered waves, secrets dwell.
With every rise, a story told,
Of ancient times and treasures bold.

The tides move in a graceful dance,
A rhythm weaving chance by chance.
Mysterious depths, a shroud of ink,
In every surge, we stop and think.

Rippling echoes of past despair,
Caress the shore with steady care.
Yet in the blue, hope's light will gleam,
A shimmer bright within the dream.

In twilight's reign, the waters sigh,
Enigmatic tides that never die.
From dusk till dawn, their stories weave,
A tapestry in which we believe.

Sable Waters

Where sable waters kiss the shore,
The twilight beckons, asking for more.
In dusk's embrace, the world holds breath,
As time meanders close to death.

Shadows stretch across the sand,
In silence, dreams take shape and stand.
Reflections dance on liquid night,
With echoes soft, they hide from light.

The lingering tunes of evening's sigh,
Invite the stars to take the sky.
In every wave, a secret lies,
As whispers blend with distant cries.

Sable waters, deep and wide,
Hold their stories with great pride.
In their depths, the future waits,
As we traverse life's twisted fates.

Secrets of the Twilight Ocean

Beneath the waves, whispers hide,
In shadows deep where secrets bide.
The currents dance with ancient lore,
While moonlight casts on the ocean's floor.

Creatures glide through sapphire dreams,
In hushed tones where silence seems.
Mysteries swirl in the salty breeze,
As twilight wraps the world with ease.

Coral gardens pulse and sway,
Guardians of the night and day.
Each wave a tale waiting to unfold,
In the twilight's heart, stories told.

Glistening pearls of wisdom bright,
Dance with stars in the velvet night.
Secrets woven in ocean's embrace,
Reveal their truths in a gentle trace.

Dark Waters, Bright Stars

In the depth of night, shadows creep,
Dark waters whisper, secrets keep.
Stars above with fervent light,
Twinkle softly, merging with night.

Ripples dance on a silken sea,
Echoes of dreams yet to be.
The horizon glows with twinkling eyes,
As moonbeams weave through starlit skies.

Beneath the veil of darkness deep,
Fish dart like thoughts we long to keep.
In the mystery of twilight's hold,
The beauty of night starts to unfold.

With each breath of the calming tide,
We find our fears begin to slide.
Dark waters cradle hopes afar,
In their depths, shine bright the stars.

The Elegance of Nightfall

As daylight fades to softest gray,
The curtains of night begin to sway.
With grace, the stars take up their place,
In the quiet calm, we find our space.

Gentle breezes rustle leaves,
Nature whispers, the night retrieves.
Shadows glide with a velvet touch,
As the world slows, it means so much.

Silhouettes dance against the moon,
A lullaby sweet, a soft tune.
Peace envelops the weary soul,
In the stillness, we become whole.

Embrace the night, let worries cease,
In every heartbeat, find your peace.
The elegance of nightfall reigns,
With promise of light in dark terrains.

Beyond the Tidal Line

Where land and ocean gently meet,
The tidal line, a realm discreet.
Footprints fade in the shifting sand,
While nature's secrets shift and expand.

Waves break softly, secrets pour,
An endless dance upon the shore.
Shells and treasures left behind,
Stories of the sea entwined.

The horizon stretches, dreams take flight,
In the golden glow of fading light.
Each ebb and flow a tale expressed,
In nature's rhythm, we find rest.

Beyond the tidal line, we stand,
Awash in wonders, time unplanned.
The universe whispers, hearts entwine,
In the magic found beyond the line.

Enchanted Ripples

In the glade where shadows play,
The water sparkles, bright and gay.
Every droplet holds a song,
Nature's chorus, sweet and strong.

Leaves flutter down like whispered dreams,
Caught in sunlight's golden beams.
Rippling water tells a tale,
Of hidden paths beyond the vale.

Mossy stones and gentle flow,
Secrets that the wild things know.
A dance of light upon the stream,
Awakens every fleeting dream.

In these moments, joy we find,
Nature's beauty, so unconfined.
Each enchanted ripple sings,
Of love and life and simple things.

Echoed Whispers

In the night where silence reigns,
Whispers travel soft like trains.
Secrets linger in the air,
Hushed confessions everywhere.

Moonlit shadows dance and sway,
Guiding hearts that lose their way.
Echoes of a distant past,
In the stillness, shadows cast.

Softly spoken, tenderly shared,
Every truth laid bare, unpaired.
In the dark, our voices blend,
In whispered hopes that never end.

Echoed tales beneath the stars,
Joining souls from near and far.
In whispered love, we find our song,
In this silence, we belong.

Depths of Solitude

In the quiet, shadows creep,
In solitude, my thoughts run deep.
A gentle hush surrounds my mind,
In this stillness, solace find.

Time flows slowly, moments blend,
In this space, I can transcend.
Each heartbeat echoes in the void,
Fears and dreams alike destroyed.

Here, the world fades into gray,
Yet, in silence, I learn to play.
With every breath, I drift away,
In solitude, I find my way.

Depths of self begin to show,
In quietude, my spirit grows.
Embraced by shadows, I stand tall,
In solitude, I hear the call.

Reflections at Twilight

When twilight bathes the sky in hues,
Reflections glimmer, soft and true.
The day retreats, replaced by calm,
Nature whispers, sweet and warm.

Shadows stretch and colors blend,
In this moment, time can bend.
Water mirrors the fading light,
Bringing dreams to life at night.

The horizon blushes, softly sighs,
As day bids farewell, the night complies.
Stars awaken, twinkling bright,
Guiding souls into the night.

At twilight's edge, we pause and see,
A reflection of what's meant to be.
In glowing dusk, our worries fade,
In this embrace, hope is laid.

Starlit Cascades

Beneath the night's vast dome,
Silver streams of light do roam.
Whispers soft in twilight fade,
Nature's song in dreams cascades.

Moonbeams dance on gentle waves,
Creating paths where silence braves.
Every shimmer tells a tale,
Of distant worlds and winds that sail.

In the hush, the echoes fall,
Flowing tunes, a whispered call.
Each cascade reflects the sky,
As time slips by, oh so sly.

Glimmers weave in darkness deep,
Awakening the stars from sleep.
In this night, beauty remains,
In starlit cascades, joy regains.

Nocturnal Breezes

Softly blows the evening air,
Whispers secrets with a flair.
Through the trees, the shadows play,
In the night, they drift away.

Crickets croon their lullabies,
Underneath the starry skies.
Gentle sways of moonlit leaves,
Nocturnal breeze, a heart that believes.

Carrying dreams on wings of night,
Guided by the silver light.
Every sigh, a silver thread,
Bound by hopes that gently spread.

In the calm, the world does cease,
Finding solace, finding peace.
With each breath, we dance and sway,
Chasing twilight 'til break of day.

Chasing Reflections

In a glassy mirror's hue,
Echoes of a sky so blue.
Images of what once was,
Whisper softly without cause.

Shadows linger on the shore,
Footprints left, forevermore.
Chasing dreams that light the way,
Fleeting moments, here to stay.

Ripples form, a gentle sigh,
Tales of time, we can't deny.
Every wave a story told,
In reflections, truths unfold.

Through this lens, the heart can see,
What it is to simply be.
Chasing reflections, we unite,
In the calm, we find our light.

Mystic Depths

In the waters, shadows blend,
Mystic depths, where dreams ascend.
Tides that pull, the heart's embrace,
Secrets sink in time and space.

Echoes ripple through the night,
Stories lost, concealed from sight.
Every glance a deeper quest,
Searching for the hidden rest.

With each wave, a whispered name,
In this realm, we're never same.
Drifting through the silken blue,
Ancient songs will guide us through.

Depths that hold both dark and light,
Illuminate the endless night.
In mystic waters, we explore,
Finding what we're searching for.

Twilight's Secrets

Soft whispers in the gloam,
As shadows start to weave,
Stars begin to find their home,
In fabric of the eve.

Crimson hues in fading light,
Day bids a sweet farewell,
Moon rises in gentle flight,
With stories left to tell.

Echoes dance on silver streams,
Where secrets linger low,
Dreams unfold in twilight's beams,
A world wrapped in soft glow.

Nature's song begins to play,
In hues of dusk divine,
While mystery leads the way,
To realms where shadows shine.

Embrace of the Deep

Beneath the azure waves, so deep,
Where sunlight dares not tread,
Silent whispers cradle sleep,
In the ocean's bed.

Coral castles rise and fall,
In currents warm and bright,
Creatures flicker, heed the call,
Of the tranquil night.

Secrets wrapped in salt and foam,
Where time forgets to flow,
The sea, it cradles all who roam,
In its gentle glow.

An embrace both fierce and kind,
In depths where dreams reside,
A world where solace you will find,
And all your fears subside.

Beneath a Shimmering Veil

Stars scattered like little pearls,
On velvet skies so wide,
Moonlight casts its silver swirls,
With secrets you can't hide.

Whispers float on gentle breeze,
Through leaves that sway and sigh,
Nature sings with perfect ease,
As night embraces sky.

In shadows lies a soft embrace,
A dance of dreams anew,
Time slows down, it finds its place,
In midnight's gentle hue.

Beneath the veil, a truth unfolds,
Of love, of hope, of light,
In every heart, a story holds,
As stars ignite the night.

The Night's Reflection

In stillness wrapped, the night appears,
A mirror to our soul,
It echoes softly all our fears,
While granting us control.

The moon, a guardian up high,
Illuminates the way,
As shadows dance and gently fly,
In dark where dreams can sway.

Each twinkle holds a whispered spark,
Of moments lost in time,
With every thought we seek to mark,
A rhythm, a gentle rhyme.

So take a breath and let it in,
The night's reflection glows,
With every loss, there's room to win,
In twilight's soft repose.

Beneath the Silent Surface

Beneath the silent surface, calm,
Life whispers softly in the depths,
Where shadows dance in meek embrace,
And secrets linger, drawing breath.

Gentle ripples cradle dreams,
Floating softly, lost to time,
In the stillness of the blue,
Life's rhythm pulses, pure and prime.

Coral gardens bloom and sway,
Beneath the gaze of watchful eyes,
Each creature plays its hidden role,
In the silence where beauty lies.

Beneath the silent surface, found,
Infinity stirs, bold and bright,
In this realm of deep delight,
A world untouched by day or sound.

The Unseen Horizon

Beyond the edge where sky meets land,
The unseen horizon stretches wide,
A canvas painted with dreams untold,
Where wanderers seek and hearts abide.

Whispers of the wind invite,
Each journey calls, each path unknown,
In the twilight's soft embrace,
Adventure lies beneath the stone.

Footprints lead to distant shores,
Where hopes and fears may intertwine,
Guided by the stars above,
We chase the light, we chase the divine.

The unseen horizon beckons still,
A promise of the bright of day,
With every step toward the dawn,
We find ourselves along the way.

The Lure of the Night

In shadows deep, the night unfolds,
A velvet cloak of mystery spun,
Stars ignite like scattered dreams,
Guiding hearts, inviting fun.

Beneath the moon's enchanting glow,
Whispers dance on the cool, still air,
Promises made with every sigh,
Secrets woven, threadbare and rare.

The nightingale sings her lullaby,
While shadows sway in gentle tune,
The world asleep, yet wide awake,
In the grasp of the silver moon.

The lure of the night pulls us near,
Into the depths of an endless maze,
With every heartbeat, we surrender,
Lost in the magic of dark displays.

Secrets in the Foam

Upon the shore where waves collide,
Whispers rise and fall like dreams,
The ocean's secrets wrapped in foam,
Voices carried on salt-laden beams.

Each bubble bursts with tales of old,
Of sailors brave, of treasures lost,
The tempest roars as fables swirl,
In every crest, our hearts are tossed.

Dancing lightly on the tide,
Footprints traced in shifting sand,
With every wave, we seek to find,
The stories lost, the ocean's hand.

Secrets in the foam confide,
In buoyant whispers, soft and clear,
The ocean speaks in timeless truth,
Echoing tales we long to hear.

Ocean's Quietude

Gentle waves caress the shore,
Whispers of the sea's soft lore.
Underneath the starlit skies,
Peaceful dreams in solace rise.

Seagulls cry in distant flight,
Moonlit paths of silver light.
Shells and sand in harmony,
Tales of time, a symphony.

Rhythmic tides that ebb and flow,
Nature's dance, a calming show.
In this quietude we find,
A sanctuary for the mind.

Here our hearts learn to be still,
Lost in waves, a tranquil thrill.
Ocean's hush, our souls align,
In her depths, we intertwine.

Reflections of the Heart

In the mirror of the soul,
Feelings deep and thoughts unroll.
Love and loss, the ties that bind,
Echoes of what's left behind.

Tender whispers in the night,
Shadows dance with faded light.
Memories like rivers flow,
Carving paths through joy and woe.

Each heartbeat a story told,
In the warmth, in the cold.
Fragments glisten, softly gleam,
Lifetimes woven in a dream.

Through the tears and laughter shared,
In the depths, our spirits bared.
Reflections haunt and yet inspire,
Every moment fuels the fire.

The Solitary Voyager

On the horizon, distant lands,
Dreams unfurl in steady hands.
Footprints traced on sandy shores,
An endless quest, it longs for more.

Stars above, a guiding light,
Whispers of the winds take flight.
Each wave has a story to tell,
In solitude, the heart can dwell.

Adventures call, a siren's song,
Through the night, I sail along.
The sea embraces, wild and free,
A journey carved in mystery.

Yet in stillness, found I grace,
In the vastness, a sacred space.
The solitary path gives way,
To deeper truths within the sway.

Nebulous Waters

In the mist, where shadows creep,
Whispers of the deep sea sleep.
Ethereal forms dance and glide,
Secrets held where dreams reside.

Glistening pearls in twilight's grasp,
Fleeting moments, time's soft clasp.
Ripples weave through veils of gray,
A world unseen, yet on display.

Caught between the night and day,
Nebulous hues in bright array.
Distant echoes call my name,
In their depths, I play the game.

Here, enchantment knows no bounds,
In the silence, magic sounds.
Nebulous waters, deep and vast,
In their embrace, my spirit's cast.

Mysterious Currents

Whispers of the deep sea flow,
Echoes in the undertow.
Secrets hidden in the tide,
Nature's pulse, a silent guide.

Waves that curl with tales untold,
Memories in blue and gold.
Carried by the ocean's grace,
Time dissolves in that vast space.

Bubbles rise, a dance so free,
Life unfolds beneath the sea.
In the depths, a world unknown,
Magic lives where light has shone.

Mysterious currents pull and sway,
Drawing hearts that drift away.
In those depths, we seek and find,
A connection forever twined.

The Soft Veil of Night

Stars begin their gentle glow,
In the sky, a silken show.
Moonlight weaves a soothing spell,
In the night, all is well.

Whispers of the evening breeze,
Stirring softly through the trees.
Shadows dance on silver streams,
Carrying our quiet dreams.

Crickets sing their lullaby,
While the world drifts softly by.
Wrapped in nighttime's tender cloak,
Every fear and worry broke.

Beneath this vast and starry dome,
In night's embrace, we find our home.
A world asleep, so calm and right,
Lost within the soft veil of night.

Driftwood Dreams

Upon the shore, what stories lie,
In pieces of wood that gently sigh.
Worn by waves and the sand's caress,
Each thread of time a soft caress.

Molded by tides and storms of the past,
Whispers of moments that forever last.
In the grain, a tale is spun,
A journey's end, a life begun.

Sheltered under the sun's warm kiss,
Fragments of nature's fleeting bliss.
In driftwood dreams, we seek to find,
A mirror of our hearts and mind.

With every wave, a memory clear,
Brought to shore, forever near.
In these tokens, love redeems,
Life's essence held in driftwood dreams.

A Dance with the Moon

Underneath the silver glow,
Softly, gently, feelings flow.
In the night, where shadows play,
We embrace the soft ballet.

With every step, the stars align,
In this moment, hearts entwine.
Whispers of a yearning tune,
Lost within our dance with the moon.

Twilight dressed in shades of blue,
Guiding us to something new.
In her light, our spirits soar,
Dancing on the ocean's floor.

Round and round, the world stands still,
As we let the night fulfill.
Lost in time, we waltz in tune,
Forever dance with the moon.

Echoes in the Stillness

Whispers dance on twilight air,
Memories linger, soft and rare.
In the quiet, shadows play,
Time slips gently, fades away.

A heartbeat in the fading light,
Silence sings of softened night.
Every sigh, a story told,
Echoes shimmer, blue and gold.

Stars awaken, one by one,
The world holds breath, night's just begun.
In the stillness, secrets weave,
Promises that night will leave.

With every rustle, dreams take flight,
Lost in depths of velvet night.
In the calm, we find our way,
Echoes linger, softly sway.

Night's Velvet Embrace

In the deep where shadows blend,
Night's embrace is like a friend.
Gentle stars begin to gleam,
Wrapped in darkness, peace is stream.

A cool breath whispers through the trees,
Carried softly by the breeze.
Crickets sing their lullaby,
While the moonlight starts to fly.

Dreamers wander, thoughts set free,
In night's grip, we cease to be.
Hands held tight, we drift away,
Time stands still, and night will stay.

Through the silence, secrets bloom,
In the quiet, hearts resume.
Within the dusk, we find our place,
Lost forever in night's grace.

Invisible Surf

Waves that crash but leave no mark,
Underneath the starlit dark.
Whispers rise and fall like tides,
In the void where silence hides.

Footsteps trace along the sand,
Written verses by unseen hand.
Ebb and flow, the dance of night,
A rhythm born from hidden light.

Ghostly echoes of the sea,
Songs of longing, set us free.
Gentle pull of dreams offshore,
Calling us to seek for more.

In this space, we lose our fears,
Invisible surf, washed in tears.
Yet each wave that breaks in sighs,
Tells of love that never dies.

Dusk's Lost Stories

As the sun sinks, shadows creep,
Tales buried deep, secrets steep.
Fading light in amber hues,
Whispers write the evening news.

Leaves crunch softly underfoot,
Each step echoes, memories put.
Stories held in twilight's grace,
Dusk reveals their hidden face.

In the glow where day meets night,
Forgotten dreams take wing in flight.
Gentle sighs of moments past,
Dusk unveils what long will last.

Gather 'round, the stories call,
In the stillness, we find all.
Lost in time, we roam and play,
Dusk's lost stories, here to stay.

Twilight's Heartbeat

In shades of violet, the skies embrace,
Whispers of dreams in a silent space.
The sun dips low, painting the night,
Stars awaken, glowing bright.

Cool breezes dance, a gentle sigh,
Carrying secrets from days gone by.
Heartbeats echo, soft and clear,
In twilight's arms, all is near.

A world transformed in dusky hues,
Time stands still, lost in views.
Moments linger, sweet and rare,
Held in twilight's tender care.

As night unfolds, we find our place,
In the echo of this quiet space.
Together we dream, together we stay,
In twilight's heartbeat, come what may.

A Song Beneath the Stars

Under the canopy where shadows play,
A melody whispers, drifting away.
Notes like fireflies dance in the night,
Singing the stories of love and light.

The moon hangs low, a watchful eye,
While constellations weave their sigh.
Harmony weaves through the veil so thin,
A song of the heart, where we begin.

Moments collide in the starlit glow,
We twirl through dreams, letting go.
Each note a promise, each chord a wish,
Beneath the stars, we find our bliss.

In whispers soft, the night unfolds,
As secrets and stories through starlight told.
In this sacred space where shadows part,
We dance to the rhythm of a hopeful heart.

Surfacing Dreams

When whispers of dawn dance on the tide,
Waves of silver, where wishes ride.
Dreams awaken, reaching for light,
Surfacing softly, taking flight.

The ocean hums a familiar tune,
As dawn breaks softly, under the moon.
Hearts drift gently on the breeze,
In the currents of hope, we seize.

Each ripple carries a tale untold,
Of courage found, and dreams bold.
With each wave that kisses the shore,
We find the strength to dream once more.

In the embrace of the rising sun,
We gather together, two become one.
Surfacing dreams in golden rays,
Together stepping into new days.

The Twilight Cascade

A cascade of colors, a breathtaking sight,
Where day whispers softly its goodnight.
The horizon blushes, a painter's brush,
In twilight's embrace, all life's a hush.

Cascading whispers through leaves on high,
Echoes of laughter, time passing by.
Golden and crimson, the clouds take flight,
A dance of shadows in fading light.

Softly the stars begin to gleam,
In the quiet of dusk, we weave a dream.
Each moment a treasure, each glance a gift,
In twilight's cascade, our spirits lift.

As day surrenders to night's gentle kiss,
We find our hearts in a world of bliss.
In the twilight cascade, hand in hand,
Together we wander, together we stand.

Shadows Dance on the Water

Whispers of the evening air,
Shadows glide with silent grace.
Moonlight weaves through every pair,
Reflecting the night's embrace.

Ripples spark in soft delight,
Dreams unfold in gentle sway.
As the stars adorn the night,
They guide the lost, come what may.

The water holds a secret song,
Melodies drift, both sweet and bright.
Carried by currents, they belong,
In the depths of the calm night.

With each ripple, life does wane,
Yet beauty dances on the tide.
In this moment, joy and pain,
Together in the shadows glide.

Celestial Ripples at Dusk

As the sun dips low and shy,
Colors paint the evening sky.
Stars emerge, their flickers tease,
Crickets chirp with gentle ease.

Rippling waters softly hum,
Echoes from a distant drum.
Moonlight spills like liquid gold,
Tales of ancient dreams retold.

The horizon blushes deep,
Veils of twilight cradle sleep.
Every wave a whispered thought,
In this magic, hope is caught.

Celestial wonders on display,
Nature's canvas on display.
In these ripples, peace I find,
A sanctuary for the mind.

Nightfall's Serenade

Beneath a cloak of velvet skies,
Stars gather in a soft reprise.
The moon hums a lullaby,
As shadows weave and gently fly.

Whispers travel on the breeze,
Carrying tales of ancient trees.
The world pauses, breath held tight,
In this serenade, pure delight.

Past the horizon's quiet line,
Night spins tales, both deep and fine.
Each rustle holds a secret close,
In the dusk, our dreams engross.

When the dark begins to rise,
There's magic lingering in the skies.
In nightfall's arms, we lay our trust,
In the velvet night, we find our just.

The Ocean's Veiled Nocturne

Waves whisper secrets on the shore,
Carrying stories from afar.
In the mist, the night does pour,
A symphony beneath each star.

Veils of fog wrap sea and night,
Mysterious, soft, a hidden sight.
The ocean hums a timeless tale,
In its depths, dreams prevail.

Moonlit paths on water dance,
Underneath, the spirits prance.
Each ripple charms the restless mind,
In this nocturne, peace we find.

Tides embrace the world anew,
In this moment, hearts are true.
The ocean and the night entwined,
In their grasp, our souls aligned.

Secrets of the Starlit Sea

Whispers dance on waves of light,
Beneath the moon's soft, silver bite.
Stars twinkle in the ocean's embrace,
Carrying tales of a distant place.

Secrets hidden in depths so deep,
Treasures that the old mermaids keep.
Songs of the sailors lost in the tide,
Echoing gently, no need to hide.

Chasing the Narrows of Night

In shadows where the night unfolds,
Dreams awaken, tales retold.
Stars weave paths through velvet dark,
Guiding hearts with a silent spark.

Whispers ride the midnight air,
Promises made in shadows rare.
Each corner turned, a mystery,
Unraveled in the quiet sea.

Where the Sea Meets the Sky

Horizons blend in hues so bright,
Where the sea kisses the sky good night.
Waves crashing tell their timeless lore,
As gulls circle, forevermore.

The sun dips low, painting streams,
Awakening the harbor of dreams.
Seaglass glints with tales untold,
In this realm where magic unfolds.

Midnight's Luminous Caress

In midnight's arms, the world unfolds,
As silver dreams break silence bold.
The stars cascade like whispers sweet,
In a dance where dark and light meet.

Gentle breezes hold secrets tight,
As the waves serenade the night.
Each ripple carries a glimmered rhyme,
A lullaby lost in the sands of time.

Luminescent Dreams of the Deep

In shadows deep, where visions glide,
A dance of light, the dreams reside.
Soft whispers call from coral spires,
Where luminescent hope conspires.

Beneath the waves, a secret blooms,
In vibrant hues, the darkness looms.
Each heartbeat sings of worlds unseen,
Where wishes float in waters green.

As currents weave a tale so grand,
The ocean cradles dreams in hand.
With every pulse, the spirits rise,
In luminescent, starry skies.

Awake, they twirl in night's embrace,
A journey bold through time and space.
In depths of dark, their colors gleam,
These luminescent dreams we dream.

Melodies of the Night's Tide

The moonlight dances on the sea,
With whispered notes, a symphony.
Each wave cascades, a soft refrain,
As night unveils its rich domain.

The stars align, a cosmic choir,
In harmony, their voices higher.
A lullaby in ocean's sway,
That carries hearts, then slips away.

The breezes hum through swaying trees,
Where shadows drape with gentle ease.
In moments lost, so sweet, so bright,
The melodies wrap the deepened night.

With every sigh, the world stands still,
As night's tide pulls with tender will.
Embraced by sounds, we drift along,
In melodies, we find our song.

Reflections in Twilight Waters

The twilight glows a soft embrace,
As ripples form a fleeting trace.
Mirrored hues of orange and gold,
In stillness, silent stories told.

The water breathes with whispered grace,
A tranquil world, a gentle space.
With every glance, the shadows play,
In fading light, they slip away.

Each moment caught in twilight's net,
A dance of light we shan't forget.
In tranquil depths, our dreams align,
Reflections spin, as stars entwine.

Let's linger here, where time stands still,
The twilight waters, the heart's soft fill.
In the calm of dusk, we softly pine,
In reflections deep, our souls entwine.

The Calm Before the Dawn

In silence deep, the world holds breath,
Awaiting light that conquers death.
The stars dim softly, one by one,
As night resigns to the rising sun.

A hush prevails, the shadows cease,
As whispers fade, and stillness speaks.
The air is thick with dreams untold,
In darkness woven, threads of gold.

The horizon blushes, faintly glows,
While nature waits for morning's shows.
Each heartbeat thrums with hopeful grace,
In calm before the dawn we trace.

Soon light will break o'er hill and vale,
As night surrenders, brief and frail.
In that calm pause, we find our way,
Embraced by promise of the day.

Whispering Shadows

In the twilight glow, whispers creep,
Shadows dance where secrets sleep.
Leaves murmur tales of the night,
Beneath the stars, soft and bright.

Flickering lights pulse through the trees,
Carried on a hushed, gentle breeze.
Echoes of dreams in the cool night air,
With every breath, enchantments flare.

Misty tendrils curl and sway,
Inviting thoughts of the end of day.
In the silence, magic quakes,
As the darkness softly wakes.

A world reborn beneath moon's kiss,
In the shadows lies untold bliss.
Take a step, embrace the dark,
In the quiet, find your spark.

Dark Currents

Beneath the surface, shadows churn,
The pulse of night begins to turn.
Whispers float on an unseen wave,
In the depths, the heart is brave.

Silent currents pull and sway,
Guiding dreams that drift away.
Rippling echoes of what has been,
Haunting the realms that lie unseen.

With every breath, a story flows,
The river knows what darkness shows.
Late at night, the secrets churn,
In darkened waters, souls will yearn.

With courage found in the swirling tide,
Embrace the depths where hopes abide.
For in these dark and quiet streams,
Lies the magic of our dreams.

Moonlit Ripples

Beneath the moon, the waters gleam,
Ripples dance like a waking dream.
Soft reflections on the lake,
Whispers of wishes, tender ache.

Silvery beams weave through the night,
Stirring the heart with pure delight.
Gentle waves kiss the shore,
Singing songs of evermore.

In the stillness, peace does bloom,
Nature's breath dispels the gloom.
Rippling echoes in the dark,
Bring forth joy with each small spark.

Allow the night to fill your soul,
In the ripples, feel the whole.
With the moon's soft, guiding light,
You are free to take your flight.

The Night's Embrace

In the hush of night, shadows grow,
The stars twinkle, soft and low.
Wrapped in silence, dreams take flight,
Cradled in the arms of night.

Glistening dew on blades of grass,
Moments linger, too sweet to pass.
Whispers linger on the breeze,
As the darkness aims to please.

Lost in wonder, hearts unite,
Under the gaze of the gentle light.
Every breath is a tender sigh,
In the night's embrace, we fly.

Let go of the burdens carried forth,
In this stillness, find your worth.
For in the night, we shall find grace,
And in our dreams, a warm embrace.

The Siren's Call

In the depths where shadows play,
A haunting melody does sway.
Whispers wrapped in silken night,
Draw sailors close with ghostly light.

Tales of love and tragic fate,
Drawn to shores where dreams await.
Lured by voices soft and sweet,
Into the waves, they find retreat.

Through the mist, her laughter flows,
A promise wrapped in silent throes.
But caution, hearts that yearn for more,
May find themselves on darker shores.

The ocean's song, a sweetened snare,
With every note, a whispered prayer.
Yet those who chase the siren's call,
May never return at all.

Echoes of the Abyss

In depths where light dares not to tread,
Ancient songs of sorrow spread.
Whispers from the ocean floor,
Call to souls who've gone before.

Silent shadows, drifting slow,
Guard the secrets only they know.
Ghostly figures swim and weave,
In the silence, hearts believe.

Tales of ships that vanished deep,
Lost in waters dark and steep.
Echoes linger, lost yet free,
In the arms of the deep blue sea.

Will you heed their mournful cry,
As the waves sing lullabies?
For those who linger, fate is sealed,
In the depths, their hearts revealed.

Starfall in the Sea

When twilight dims and stars align,
The ocean glimmers like fine wine.
Beneath the waves, a dance so bright,
Whispers of magic, pure delight.

Falling stars meet the gentle tide,
Where dreams and waters do collide.
Each sparkle tells a tale anew,
Of wishes cast, of hopes so true.

Cradled by the sea's embrace,
Luminous trails leave not a trace.
Beneath the ripples, dreams take flight,
In the heart of the starry night.

When dawn arrives, the magic fades,
But echoes of the night cascades.
In every wave that sings a tune,
Lies the mystery of the moon.

Dances of the Dark

In moonlit realms where shadows prance,
The night reveals its secret dance.
Whispers twirl on midnight air,
As stars become the dancers' glare.

Glimmers flicker, soft and low,
With every step, the dark does glow.
Silhouette of dreams unfurled,
In this hushed and mystic world.

Echoes linger, sounds of grace,
As night embraces every space.
Beneath the cloak of twilight's veil,
Each spirit sways, a ghostly trail.

So come and join the shadows' waltz,
Where light retreats, and darkness vaults.
In the stillness, find your spark,
For life awaits in dances dark.

Silhouette of the Tide

Whispers dance on the ebbing flow,
Shadows stretch where the breezes blow.
Footprints fade on the sandy shore,
As twilight calls, we seek for more.

The sun dips low, painted in gold,
Secrets wrapped in the night unfold.
Waves return with a gentle sigh,
In the fading light, our dreams comply.

Stars awaken, the horizon gleams,
The moonlit path reveals our dreams.
Each crest and trough, a tale untold,
In the tide's embrace, we find our hold.

As night unfurls its velvet sheets,
The silhouette of love repeats.
Together here, where shadows glide,
We lose ourselves in the ocean's tide.

Moon's Embrace on Silent Shores

Beneath the silver glow so bright,
The moonlit waves dance in the night.
Whispers of seashells, soft and low,
Carried by tides, where dreams can flow.

A gentle breeze through palm trees sways,
Where the sandy beach in silence lays.
Each wave that breaks, a heartfelt sound,
As starlit hopes in the dark rebound.

Footprints marked on the ocean's rim,
Memories cling, though they may dim.
In the moon's embrace, we feel the grace,
Of nature's love in this tranquil space.

Together we watch, the night awake,
As dreams of the sea, together we take.
With hands entwined, hearts softly soar,
On silent shores, forevermore.

Dreaming in Aquatic Night

In depths of blue where shadows play,
We drift and dream, let the night sway.
The ocean calls with a siren's song,
Together here, we feel we belong.

Photos of fish in colors bright,
Illuminate the depths of night.
Around the coral, a dance is spun,
Beneath the waves, our hearts are one.

Glow of the stars through water beams,
Flowing gently in the silver streams.
As we dive deeper, secrets unfurl,
In the aquatic night, we find our world.

Rising bubbles break the dream,
Transforming thoughts into a gleam.
In the sea's embrace, we lose our fright,
Forever locked in aquatic night.

Secrets Beneath the Surface

Hidden wonders lie far below,
In shadows where the moonbeams glow.
Secrets whisper in currents swift,
As the ocean's depths, our hearts uplift.

With every wave, a story waits,
Ancient tales through the water's gates.
Life teems in silence, a world apart,
In the depths, there lies a beating heart.

Each ripple speaks of years gone by,
In the stillness where the fish glide by.
Echos linger in a watery space,
A hidden realm, a sacred place.

Diving down where the sun can't reach,
We learn the lessons that oceans teach.
In secrets deep, we find our fate,
Beneath the surface, we contemplate.

Hidden Horizons

Beyond the hills where silence lies,
Dreams awaken under painted skies.
Secrets whisper in the gentle breeze,
As shadows dance among the trees.

The sun dips low, a fiery glow,
Where love once thrived, now soft and slow.
Echoes linger of laughter past,
In hidden places where moments cast.

Paths unseen invite the brave,
Each step a journey, a chance to save.
In twilight's hush, the heart will roam,
Finding solace, a place called home.

With every horizon that fades from sight,
Hope unfurls like wings in flight.
In the embrace of night's sweet grace,
We seek the dawn, a warm embrace.

Glimmering Abyss

Beneath the waves, the secrets dwell,
In watery depths, an ancient spell.
Lights dance softly, a magnetic pull,
Where shadows linger, rich and full.

In the glimmering abyss, dreams converge,
Whispers of the ocean, a timeless urge.
Colorful creatures in a twilight haze,
Guide the lost through the murky maze.

Echoes of silence, soft as a sigh,
As currents swirl and stars drift by.
Each moment a treasure, delicate, rare,
In the depths of the ocean, life laid bare.

Awash in mystery, we plunge and dive,
In the heart of the dark, we learn to thrive.
With every pulse, the sea will reveal,
The wonders hidden, the truth we feel.

Celestial Undercurrents

Stars twinkle bright in the velvet night,
Whispers of cosmos in ethereal flight.
Dreamers wander on stardust trails,
Through celestial paths, where magic prevails.

Each flicker tells of journeys untold,
Of ancient tales in the starlight's fold.
Luna's embrace, a gentle guide,
Through galaxies vast where dreams abide.

In the stillness, a heartbeat blends,
With the rhythm of time as the universe bends.
Galaxies swirl in a cosmic dance,
Each moment a note in existence's trance.

As meteors streak and comets soar,
We are but travelers, forever exploring more.
In celestial undercurrents, we find our way,
Connecting the night to the light of day.

Twilight's Echo

When daylight fades, a soft embrace,
Painting the skies with a warm, rich grace.
In that hush, the world slows down,
As night wraps gently around the town.

Whispers linger in shadows cast,
Memories echo, both tender and fast.
Under the blanket of glittering stars,
We trace the stories etched in our scars.

Twilight's glow a fleeting friend,
In its silence, our hearts can mend.
With fireflies dancing, dreams ignite,
In the softest corners of the night.

Embrace the twilight, let worries flee,
In this sacred moment, just you and me.
For in the echoes of the fading light,
We find our solace until the night.

Milton Keynes UK
Ingram Content Group UK Ltd.
UKHW052022251024
450245UK00012B/637

9 789916 908310